COGNITIVE BEHAVIOURAL THERAPY SOCIAL ANXIETY

Understanding and Overcoming Social Anxiety Through CBT

Jane C. Sheehan

Copyright © 2023

All Rights Are Reserved

The content in this book may not be reproduced, duplicated, or transferred without the express written permission of the author or publisher. Under no circumstances will the publisher or author be held liable or legally responsible for any losses, expenditures, or damages incurred directly or indirectly as a consequence of the information included in this book.

Legal Remarks

Copyright protection applies to this publication. It is only intended for personal use. No piece of this work may be modified, distributed, sold, quoted, or paraphrased without the author's or publisher's consent.

Disclaimer Statement

Please keep in mind that the contents of this booklet are meant for educational and recreational purposes. Every effort has been made to offer accurate, up-to-date, reliable, and thorough information. There are, however, no stated or implied assurances of any kind. Readers understand that the author is providing competent counsel. The content in this book originates from several sources. Please seek the opinion of a competent professional before using any of the tactics outlined in this book. By reading this book, the reader agrees that the author will not be held accountable for any direct or indirect damages resulting from the use of the information contained therein, including, but not limited to, errors, omissions, or inaccuracies.

TABLE OF CONTENTS

INTRODUCTION

The common and often upsetting condition of social anxiety puts a shadow over the lives of many people, making it harder for them to handle social situations without problems. This short article goes into the potential field of cognitive behavioral therapy (CBT), which is a bright light for people with social anxiety who want to get better.

Cognitive behavioral therapy for social anxiety: an introduction

The common and often upsetting condition of social anxiety puts a shadow over the lives of many people, making it harder for them to handle social situations without problems. This short article goes into the potential field of cognitive behavioral therapy (CBT), which is a bright light for people with social anxiety who want to get better.

In the next few chapters, we'll look into the different aspects of social anxiety, from where it comes from and how to diagnose it to how cognitive behavioral therapy (CBT) can help people change. This journey will take you on a look at the cognitive causes, behavioral interventions, and mindfulness methods that make up a complete way to deal with social anxiety. Come learn with us how cognitive behavioral therapy (CBT) can help people change the way they think, face their fears, and build lasting confidence in social situations. In the next few chapters, we'll look into the different aspects of social anxiety, from where it comes from and how to diagnose it to how cognitive behavioral therapy (CBT) can help people change. This journey will take you on a look at the cognitive causes, behavioral interventions, and mindfulness methods that make up a complete way to deal with social anxiety. Come learn with us how cognitive behavioral therapy (CBT) can help people change the way they think, face their fears, and build lasting confidence in social situations.

CHAPTER ONE

UNDERSTANDING SOCIAL ANXIETY

Definition and Overview of Social Anxiety

Social anxiety, which is sometimes called social phobia, is a mental illness that causes people to be very afraid of being around other people. People who have social anxiety often worry too much about being judged, embarrassed, or badly evaluated by other people. This fear can show up in a lot of different social situations, from casual chats to formal events, and it can have a big effect on both personal and work life.

A big part of social anxiety is feeling very self-conscious, which is different from being nervous in social situations. People who have social anxiety often think that bad things will happen, which makes them avoid social situations or feel very uncomfortable during them. Trying to avoid things can hurt your relationships, your performance at school or work, and your general quality of life.

Social anxiety isn't just shyness or occasional nerves; it's a pattern of constant and upsetting fear that can make it hard to go about daily life. It usually starts in childhood, but it can happen at any age. Understanding the complex nature of social anxiety is important for helping and assisting people who are experiencing it.

Prevalence and Impact of Social Anxiety

A large part of the population deals with social nervousness, which is a common mental health problem. Although the number of people who have social anxiety disorder varies by culture and age, it is thought that between 7 and 12 percent of people will have it at some point in their lives.

The teenage years are a time when social interactions and ties with peers become more important, which is also when social anxiety tends to show up more. It is normal for social anxiety symptoms to last into adulthood if they are not treated.

Someone with social anxiety can be deeply affected by it, and this can affect many areas of their lives. One of the main effects is limiting social activities and staying away from things that make you anxious. Avoidance like this can make it harder to build relationships, get ahead in your job, and feel less alone.

Social anxiety can make it hard to communicate, work together, and move up in your job, whether you're at school or at work. Some people with social anxiety has trouble with things like networking, public speaking, and doing things with a group, all of which are important parts of both school and work life.

Social anxiety can be very hard on your emotions. It can make you feel inadequate, lower your self-esteem, and make you worry constantly about future social interactions. Social anxiety can make it easier for other mental health problems to happen, like sadness and drug abuse, if it is not treated.

Knowing how common and bad social anxiety is makes it even more important to spot it early and get help for it. People with social anxiety can learn to control their fears, improve their social skills, and regain a full and socially active life by using cognitive-behavioral therapy and other types of therapy.

The Cognitive Behavioral Approach to Social Anxiety

Cognitive behavioral therapy (CBT) is one of the most important ways to handle social anxiety because it gives you a structured and evidence-based way to understand and deal with the complicated way that your thoughts, feelings, and actions are connected when you have this condition.

When it comes to social anxiety, cognitive behavioral therapy (CBT) is based on the idea that our thoughts, or cognitions, have a big effect on how we feel and act. Individuals can change their emotional reactions and, as a result, the ways they act when they have social anxiety by recognizing and changing problematic thought patterns.

Cognitive Component: Cognitive behavioral therapy (CBT) for social anxiety starts with looking at the cognitive component. This means figuring out the automatic thoughts and false beliefs that make people more anxious in social situations. People learn to recognize and question their bad self-perceptions, catastrophic thinking, and irrational fears. This helps them see things more realistically and in a more balanced way.

The behavioral part is:

The behavioral part of cognitive-behavioral therapy (CBT) looks at the avoidance and safety practices that people with social anxiety use to deal with their feelings of discomfort. People gradually face and become less sensitive to things that make them anxious by repeatedly putting themselves in social situations they fear. The goal of this method, which is called exposure treatment, is to change unwanted behaviors and boost confidence in social situations.

Putting together cognitive and behavioral strategies:

Cognitive restructuring and behavioral techniques work together in CBT. People are better prepared for social situations they are afraid of when they question and change negative thought habits. This two-pronged method not only eases immediate distress, but it also builds long-term resilience, which means that people can handle social situations with more confidence and less anxiety.

Because CBT is communal and goal-oriented, it gives people the power to take an active role in their healing process. The cognitive-behavioral technique has been shown to be a very helpful and empowering way for people with social anxiety to get better by making them more self-aware, giving them useful tools for dealing with anxiety, and encouraging them to slowly face social challenges.

CHAPTER TWO

ASSESSMENT AND DIAGNOSIS OF SOCIAL ANXIETY

Identifying Social Anxiety Symptoms

Recognizing the signs of social anxiety is an important first step in getting to know and dealing with this difficult disease. There are many ways that social anxiety symptoms can show up and affect how a person thinks, feels, and acts in social settings. To help you spot social anxiety, here are some key signs:

1. Too much fear of negative evaluation:

- A strong and constant fear of being judged, scolded, or rejected by other people.
- The fear of embarrassing oneself in public, which makes people avoid those scenarios.

2. Physical Symptoms:

- Signs of worry in the body, like shaking, sweating, blushing, or a fast heartbeat, especially when you're with other people.
- Gastrointestinal discomfort, including nausea or an upset stomach, in response to social contacts

3. Avoidance of Social Situations:

- Regularly staying away from social events, gatherings, or activities where you'll be interacting with other people

- Trouble starting or keeping talks going, even with people they know.

4. Negative self-perception:

- Having low self-esteem and believing that you are not good enough in social situations or less important than other people.

- Self-critical thoughts about what you think are your social flaws or mistakes.

5. "Overthinking and Rumination":

- Thinking and focusing too much on perceived mistakes or embarrassing events from past social interactions.

- Fear and worry about what might go wrong before social events, which can become a problem.

6. Hyper-awareness:

- Hyper-awareness of one's own physical appearance or behavior in social settings is called physical self-consciousness.

- Feeling scrutinized by others, even in the absence of objective evidence.

7. Difficulty Speaking or Performing in Public:

- Having trouble speaking or doing things in front of other people, which makes them avoid public speaking or performing situations.
- Being afraid of being seen or making a mistake in front of other people.

8. "Isolation and Loneliness":

- Removal from society and being alone because of the stress that comes with interacting with other people.
- Having trouble making and keeping personal and professional ties.

Diagnostic Criteria and Assessment Tools

There are certain criteria in the Diagnostic and Statistical Manual of Mental Disorders (DSM-5) that are used to identify social anxiety disorder. For someone to have a social anxiety disorder, they must have a lot of trouble with their social and occupational functioning because they are very afraid or anxious in one or more social settings. This is a list of ten diagnostic criteria:

1. Marked Fear or Anxiety: A strong fear or anxiety that follows a person into one or more social situations where they might be watched by others.

2. Types of avoidance: Avoidance of social situations that you don't want to be in or endurance of those situations, even though they cause you a lot of stress or worry.

3. Immediate worry response: This is the worry you feel right before going into a social situation you're afraid of.

4. Physical Symptoms: When you're in a social setting, you may experience physical symptoms like shaking, sweating, blushing, or stomach pain.

5. Social Interaction Anxiety: a strong fear of interacting with other people, like starting talks, being in small groups, or doing new things with other people.

6. Performance: Anxiety is stress that comes from having to do things like speak in public or act in front of other people.

7. Impaired Daily Life: Having social anxiety makes it hard for a person to go about their daily life, have relationships, do well in school, or do their job.

8. Exclusion of Other Conditions: The symptoms can't be explained better by the effects of a drug or another medical condition.

9. "Significant Distress or Impairment" means that the social anxiety isn't caused by a medical condition, medication, or drug abuse, and it gets in the way of important areas of working in social, occupational, or other ways.

Tests to check for social anxiety:

People who work in mental health use a number of standard tools to evaluate and rate the seriousness of social anxiety symptoms. Here are ten widely used assessment tools:

1. The Social Phobia Inventory (SPIN) is a self-report tool that measures how bad social anxiety symptoms are.

2. The Liebowitz Social Anxiety Scale (LSAS) is a questionnaire that can be given by a clinician or filled out by the person themselves to find out how much they fear and avoid social settings.

3. The Social Interaction Anxiety Scale (SIAS) is a self-report scale that is intended to measure anxiety in social situations.

4. The Social Phobia Scale (SPS) is a part of the Social Phobia and Anxiety Inventory that measures fear in social settings.

5. The Mini-Social Phobia Inventory (Mini-SPIN) is a short test for social anxiety disease.

6. Fear of Negative Evaluation Scale (FNE): This scale measures the fear of being judged negatively by other people.

7. The Social Anxiety Questionnaire for Adults (SAQ-A30) is a self-report questionnaire that looks at different parts of social anxiety in adults.

8. The Social Anxiety and Distress Scale (SADS) measures how anxious and upset people are when they are with other people.

9. Patient Health Questionnaire for Social Anxiety (PHQ-SA): This is a part of the PHQ series that checks for signs of social anxiety.

10. The Social Avoidance and Distress Scale (SADS) measures how much people avoid and feel stressed in different social settings.

Differentiating Social Anxiety from Other Disorders

1. Specificity of Fear: People with social anxiety are afraid of being judged or evaluated negatively in social situations. This is what sets it apart from people with generalized anxiety disorder, whose anxiety is more widespread.

2. Social Focus: For people with social anxiety, the main thing that makes them anxious is being around other people. People with other anxiety disorders, like panic disorder or agoraphobia, may be more worried about different situations.

3. Avoidance Patterns: People who have social anxiety often do things to avoid being in social situations. For example, people with other fears or obsessive-compulsive disorders may avoid different things because of their symptoms.

4. Performance Anxiety: This type of social anxiety is different from disorders like generalized anxiety disorder because it often includes fears of acting in public or speaking in front of other people.

5. Starts in social situations: The main thing that sets off the symptoms of social anxiety is interacting with other people. This is what makes it different from mood illnesses like depression or bipolar disorder.

6. Cognitive Patterns: People with social anxiety have certain bad thought patterns about how other people will judge them, while people with obsessive-compulsive disorder have unwanted thoughts that make them do things over and over again.

7. Physical Symptoms in Social Context: For people with social anxiety, physical symptoms like blushing, sweating, or trembling are most common in social situations. This is different from other disorders, where different scenarios can set off symptoms.

8. Interaction with Social Skills: People with social anxiety often think they are bad at social skills, while people with illnesses like schizophrenia may have trouble reading social cues.

9. Fear of Being Made Fun of: One thing that sets social anxiety apart from post-traumatic stress disorder (PTSD) is the fear of being embarrassed or humiliated. In PTSD, the fear is linked to a painful event.

10. Relationship Dynamics: Social anxiety tends to have a direct effect on relationships with other people. This is different from personality disorders, where unhealthy patterns show up in many situations.

11. Social Comparisons: People with social anxiety often compare themselves to others too much. This is different from body dysmorphic disorder, which is focused on flaws in the body.

12. Attention to Self in Social Context: People with social anxiety are more aware of themselves in social settings, while people with attention-deficit/hyperactivity disorder (ADHD) have problems with paying attention in general.

13. Specific Phobias: Social anxiety is a specific phobia, but it is different from other specific phobias like fear of heights or animals because it is more focused on social situations and fear of being judged negatively.

14. Thoughts that come back to you during obsessive-compulsive disorder In social anxiety, the main thing that makes people feel bad is being around other people. In obsessive-compulsive disorder, on the other hand, people feel bad because of unwanted thoughts that have nothing to do with other people.

15. Temporal Aspects: Social anxiety usually starts early, around puberty. This makes it different from disorders or conditions that appear later in life in response to certain events.

CHAPTER THREE

COGNITIVE MODEL OF SOCIAL ANXIETY

Cognitive Distortions and Negative Thought Patterns

Cognitive errors and negative thought patterns are big parts of keeping social anxiety going and making it worse. These distortions make it easier to believe false and often insulting things about yourself and other people in social settings. People who are getting cognitive behavioral therapy (CBT) for social anxiety need to understand these thought processes. Here are some common cognitive distortions and negative thought processes that people with social anxiety have:

Catastrophizing:

1. Thought pattern: picturing the worst thing that could happen in social settings.

Case in point: "If I say something silly during the meeting, everyone will think I'm incompetent, and I'll never be taken seriously again."

2. Mind Reading:

Thought Field: Assuming that you know what other people are thinking and generally passing judgment on them negatively.

Case in point: "They probably think I'm awkward and dull." I must be coming across badly."

As a thought pattern, all-or-nothing thinking means seeing things in black-and-white terms and not seeing the middle ground.

Case in point: "If I'm not the life of the party, I've failed miserably." There is no middle ground.

This is a thought pattern: jumping to negative conclusions about a lot of people based on little proof.

Case in point: "I messed up that presentation, as usual." That's not something I'll ever be good at.

Taking blame for outside events or other people's actions, even when it's not fair, is an example of personalization.

Case in point: "I guess they didn't laugh at my joke because I'm not funny." I made the whole night bad."

Filtering is a thought pattern in which you only think about the bad things about a situation and ignore the good things.

Case in point: "I made a small mistake during the conversation; now, everything I said is worthless, and they'll remember me for that."

Thought Pattern: Thinking that negative feelings show what is really going on in the world.

Case in point: "I feel anxious and awkward, so I must be making everyone else uncomfortable."

8. "Should Statements": "Thought Pattern": Putting strict rules or impossible goals on yourself.

Case in point: "I should always be sure of myself and never show weakness." It's a sign of weakness if I do."

Often negatively, constantly comparing oneself to others is a thought pattern called "comparison."

Case in point: "They look so comfortable around other people." I'm not as nice or interesting as they are.

Focusing only on what you think are bad cues in social situations is an example of selective attention.

Case in point: "They glanced away when I was talking; they must be bored or uninterested in what I have to say."

Automatic Thoughts in Social Situations

Automatic thoughts are quick, impulsive, and frequently subconscious ideas that come to mind in response to particular circumstances. When it comes to social anxiety, these habitual thoughts are crucial in influencing people's emotional reactions and actions. In cognitive behavioral therapy (CBT), recognizing and treating these habitual beliefs is a fundamental part of treating social anxiety. The following are typical automatic ideas that can come up in social settings:

Cognitive Distortions:

Automatic Thought: "I'm sure everyone is judging me right now."

Cognitive distortion: mind reading, or assuming the worst about somebody without providing proof.

2. Catastrophizing:

Automatic Thought: "This conversation will be disastrous if I stutter."

Illogical Belief: Catastrophizing is the act of imagining the worst-case scenario.

3. Overgeneralization:

Automatic Thought: "I always make mistakes; I've had awkward moments before."

Cognitive Distortion: Overgeneralization: making generalizations about unfavorable events

4. Personalization:

Automatic Thought: "I must be the reason behind their lack of interest in the conversation."

Illogical Belief Personalization: Assuming excessive accountability for outside circumstances

5. Selective Attention:

Automatic Thought: "I guess they thought I was boring because they looked away when I spoke."

Illogical Belief: Selective Attention: concentrating just on cues that are deemed negative.

6. Inner Reading:

Instinctive Thought: "It's likely that they perceive me as awkward and unlikeable."

Cognitive Misconception: Mind reading: thinking you know what other people are thinking.

Social Comparisons:

Automatic Thought: "Everyone else seems more interesting and self-assured than me."

Social comparisons, or negatively comparing oneself to others, are a cognitive distortion.

8. Should Declarations:

Automatic Thought: "I should always be flawless in social circumstances."

Cognitive Distortion: Should Statements: Putting oneself under excessive pressure

9. Filtering:

Automatic Thought: "The entire interaction is ruined because of a small mistake I made."

Illogical Belief: Filtering: Concentrating only on the unfavorable elements of a circumstance.

10. Emotional Reasoning:

Automatic Thought: "I think I'm nervous, so I must be causing discomfort for everyone."

Cognitive Misconception: Emotional Reasoning: The idea that feelings are a reflection of the outside world

11. Overcoming Resistance:

Automatic Thought: "I should just stay away from this situation; I can't handle it."

Assuming an inability to cope is a cognitive distortion that occurs when overcoming resistance.

Core Beliefs and Assumptions Underlying Social Anxiety

Fundamental convictions about oneself, other people, and the world that are profoundly embedded are known as core beliefs and assumptions. These fundamental ideas frequently play a major role in the emergence and maintenance of anxious cognitive patterns and actions in the context of social anxiety. One of the main components of cognitive behavioral therapy (CBT) for social anxiety is recognizing and questioning these fundamental beliefs. The following typical fundamental ideas and presumptions underlie social anxiety:

1. A Fear of Unfavorable Assessment:

Basic Belief: "I have to have everyone's approval and likeness all the time."

Assumption: An individual's value is only established by outside validation.

2. Perfectionism:

Basic Belief: "I have to be perfect in social settings; any error is offensive."

Assumption: Deviation from perfection is grounds for rejection; imperfections are not accepted.

3. Core belief: "I am fundamentally inferior to others."

Assumption: Some people are just more capable, endearing, or deserving.

4. Unconditional Acceptance:

Basic Belief: "I have to be perfect and live up to everyone's expectations in order for others to accept me."

Assumption: Fulfilling unreasonable requirements is a requirement for acceptance.

5. Catastrophic Thinking: is characterized by the core belief that "if I make a social mistake, it's a catastrophe."

Assumption: Adverse societal consequences are disastrous and unchangeable.

6. Excessive Self-Focus:

Core Belief: "I'm always being scrutinized and judged by others."

Assumption: One's own attention is mostly focused on others.

7. Social Inferiority:

Basic Belief: "I am not as socially ade pt as other people."

Assumption: Social skills are set, and it is doubtful that they will get better.

8. Rejection Sensitivity:

Basic Belief: "It is intolerable to be rejected and should be avoided by all means."

Assumption: Personal inadequacy is a direct reflection of rejection.

9. Exaggerated Responsibility:

Basic Belief: "I am accountable for other people's comfort and social reactions."

One's actions have a disproportionate effect on the feelings of other people.

10. Anticipatory Anxiety:

Core Belief: "There is never a social situation that isn't unpleasant and anxiety-inducing."

Assumption: In social interactions, bad things will always happen.

11. Avoidance as Coping:

Basic Belief: "The only way to stop anxiety is to stay out of social situations."

Assumption: Avoidance is a useful and essential anxiety management technique.

12. Overemphasis on Opinions of Others:

Basic Belief: "The opinions of others are more important than my own assessment of myself."

Assumption: One's sense of worth depends on assessments from others.

13. Comparison to Others:

Basic Belief: "I am not as smart, talented, or appealing as other people."

Assumption: Feelings of inadequacy are reinforced when someone constantly compares themselves to others.

CHAPTER FOUR

BEHAVIORAL STRATEGIES FOR SOCIAL ANXIETY

Exposure Therapy: Systematic Desensitization

A key component of cognitive behavioral therapy (CBT), or systematic desensitization, is exposure therapy for social anxiety. This research-based strategy attempts to lessen anxiety by introducing people to social settings they are afraid of step-by-step, under supervision, and in a systematic way. The method entails dismantling the hierarchy of frightening circumstances and progressively exposing the person to each level. An outline of systematic desensitization is provided below:

1. Building a Fear Structure:

Recognition: Individuals identify a hierarchy of social situations they fear, rated from least to most anxiety-inducing, in collaboration with their therapist. This hierarchy might include things like making eye contact, striking up a discussion, or speaking in front of a group of people.

2. Meditation Methods:

Relaxation Introductory: People study and practice relaxing methods prior to exposure, such as progressive muscle relaxation or deep breathing. These methods function as instruments to control anxiety while being exposed.

3. Creating the Fear Hierarchy:

Developing the Hierarchy: Together, the therapist and the subject compile a thorough list of social situations that they are afraid of. Every scenario is rated according to the anxiety level of the individual, with the least anxiety-inducing circumstances at the bottom and the most anxiety-inducing scenarios at the top.

4. Systematic Exposure:

Gradual Exposure: The person starts with the scenario that makes them feel the least anxious. Anxiety becomes ingrained through frequent, controlled exposures, and the person gets desensitized to that specific circumstance. They advance to the next level on the ladder as they gain mastery.

5. Using Cognitive Restructuring:

Recognizing and Displacing Assumptions: In the process of exposure, people also learn to recognize and confront their instinctive negative beliefs about every circumstance. Cognitive restructuring strategies are incorporated here to modify maladaptive thought patterns.

6. Encouraging and Positive Feedback:

Positive Reinforcement: The therapist gives the patient positive reinforcement, praising their efforts and advancement. This affirmation fosters self-assurance and drives for additional exposure.

7. Applicability in Real Life: Transferring Knowledge to **Real-Life Situations:** The person is encouraged to apply the techniques they have acquired in treatment to social settings in real life as they move up the fear hierarchy. This makes it easier to generalize and sustain advancement over time.

8. Review and Modification: Continuous Evaluation: Every month, the patient and the therapist evaluate the patient's progress. If the patient's anxiety level shifts or if new problems come up, the hierarchy may need to be adjusted.

Role-playing and Social Skills Training

Two important elements of cognitive behavioral therapy (CBT) for social anxiety are role-playing and social skills training. These methods give people a controlled, encouraging environment in which to hone and improve their social skills. To help you become more confident in social situations, try these 15 role-playing and social skills training exercises:

1. A Brief Overview of Fundamental Conversational Skills:

Simulation: Practice fundamental social skills, including greetings, small talk, and asking open-ended questions, by participating in scripted dialogues.

2. Exercises in Active Listening:

Play pretend: Take turns speaking and listening. To improve your active listening abilities, try paraphrasing and summarizing what the other person has said.

3. Starting and Closing Discussions:

Acting Out: Create pretend situations where people can practice striking up conversations and ending them politely. This entails making an introduction, showing attention, and drawing conclusions from a conversation in a natural way.

4. Training in Assertiveness:

Play pretend: In a safe situation, practice using assertive communication strategies such as voicing your thoughts, establishing limits, and making requests.

5. Managing Rejection and Criticism:

Acting out: Play out situations in which people are rejected or receive constructive feedback. Develop your ability to react coolly and confidently.

6. Scenarios for Conflict Resolution: Role-play: Play out situations where there are only minor disputes. Develop your ability to resolve conflicts amicably by practicing active listening and coming up with workable alternatives.

7. Skills for Group Interaction:

Play pretend: Encourage people to practice starting and joining in group discussions by simulating group environments. Pay attention to social dynamics and nonverbal cues.

8. Network Activities:

Play pretend: Practice networking situations by giving an introduction, trading contact details, and striking up business-related discussions.

9. Simulated Social Event:

Play pretend: Construct scenarios that mimic common social gatherings, such as parties. Practice going up to different people, striking up a conversation, and mingling.

10. Graduation Remarks:

Play pretend: Play out scenarios in which people are complimented. Learn how to politely accept and acknowledge compliments.

11. Practice Public Speaking:

Play pretend: Expose them to public speaking situations gradually; begin with small groups and work your way up to larger gatherings. Give your message clearly, and concentrate on controlling your nervousness.

12. Emotional Expression in Appropriate Contexts:

Act out: In a safe environment, practice expressing your feelings. This cover controlling more difficult emotions like impatience or disappointment as well as happy feelings like joy.

13. Awareness of Body Language:

Play pretend: Examine how body language affects social interactions. Make an effort to keep eye contact, use open body language, and recognize nonverbal clues from other people.

14. Handling Uncomfortable Subjects:

Acting Out: Play out scenarios with potentially sensitive subjects. Get comfortable handling these discussions with grace and confidence.

15. Establishing and Preserving Friendships:

Act-play: Examine situations pertaining to establishing, growing, and preserving friendships. Develop the abilities required to create deep connections.

Gradual Exposure and Hierarchy Building

Cognitive behavioral therapy (CBT) uses gradual exposure, frequently in conjunction with hierarchy building, as a core strategy to treat social anxiety. This methodical, regulated technique based on evidence assists people in facing and overcoming their phobias. This is a comprehensive guide on using hierarchy-building and progressive exposure to treat social anxiety.

1. Social Anxiety Assessment:

Verification: Work together with the person to pinpoint particular social circumstances that make them feel anxious. These can be situations that are somewhat upsetting or extremely anxiety-inducing.

2. Fear Hierarchy Creation:

Hierarchy Development: Create a fear hierarchy with the person by arranging the circumstances that have been identified in order of least to most anxiety-inducing. This hierarchy functions as an exposure road map.

3. Recognizing Autonomous Thoughts:

A Cognitive Investigation: Assist the person in recognizing the automatic negative thoughts connected to every scenario in the hierarchy. These ideas may be illogical convictions or anxieties about being judged, rejected, or embarrassed.

4. A Brief Overview of Relaxation Methods:

Relaxation Instruction: Instruct and put into practice relaxing methods, including progressive muscle relaxation and deep breathing. During exposure, these methods act as coping mechanisms.

5. Beginning with Low-Anxiety Situations:

Initial Exposure: Take the scenario that causes the least amount of anxiety at the bottom of the hierarchy. It is advised that the person expose themselves to this circumstance on a regular basis until their fear considerably subsides.

6. Systematic Exposure:

Repeated Exposure Sessions: As you move up the fear hierarchy, you should progressively expose yourself to more stressful situations as you get more at ease. Sessions might be planned on a regular basis to keep things moving.

7. Cognitive Restructuring Integration:

Thought-provoking: As you expose yourself, concentrate on recognizing and resisting your habitual negative thoughts. Reshape cognitive processes by introducing more realistic, alternative concepts.

8. Positive Feedback and Reinforcement:

Encouraging: At every stage of exposure, give the person praise for their efforts and achievements. Remarks ought to center on their bravery and the steady lowering of their level of fear.

9. Application in Real Life:

Overall: Promote the use of newly acquired abilities in contexts outside of therapy. People are driven to try new things in contexts that are naturally sociable.

10. Regular Evaluation and Modification:

Continuous Evaluation: Review the fear hierarchy and progress on a regular basis. Modify the hierarchy in response to shifts in anxiety levels, achievements, and potential new difficulties.

11. Social Skills Training Integration:

Skill Development: To improve interpersonal skills, combine social skills training with exposure. Exposure sessions might incorporate role-playing and practicing acceptable social behaviors.

12. Overcoming Obstacles and Difficulties:

Developing Resilience: Resolve obstacles or setbacks by applying problem-solving techniques. Urge them to see failures as chances for development and learning.

13. Combining Self-Care and Exposure:

Self-Compassion: Throughout the process, stress the value of self-care. Urge people to be kind and understanding to themselves, as well as to acknowledge and celebrate their accomplishments.

14. Long-Term Maintenance: *Prevention of Relapses: * Talk about a long-term strategy for keeping the gains going. Create a relapse prevention strategy that incorporates coping mechanisms and continuing exposure.

15. Conclusion and Analysis:

Result: As the person moves up the hierarchy and accomplishes their objectives, lead a contemplative conversation about the process. Reiterate newly acquired abilities and talk about autonomous maintenance techniques.

CHAPTER FIVE

COGNITIVE RESTRUCTURING TECHNIQUES

Identifying and Challenging Negative Thoughts

Cognitive behavioral therapy (CBT) for social anxiety includes recognizing and combating negative beliefs as a fundamental component. This procedure entails identifying automatic thought patterns that fuel worry and methodically questioning and changing them. Here's a detailed how-to:

1. Awareness of Oneself and Mindfulness:

Observation: Assist people in observing their thoughts without passing judgment. Being mindful makes it easier to recognize when unfavorable thoughts come up on autopilot.

2. Log Your Negative Thoughts:

Writing Down: Request that people maintain a thinking journal in which they log any instances of unfavorable ideas about societal circumstances. Provide specifics like the circumstances, feelings, and related ideas.

3. List Cognitive Distortions in Category:

Education: Educate people about typical cognitive distortions, such as overgeneralization, mind reading, and catastrophizing. Assist people in identifying these distortions in the thoughts they have recorded.

4. Detect Autonomous Thoughts:

Thought Surveillance: Help people recognize the automatic thoughts that are associated with social anxiety. These ideas might be catastrophic, self-critical, or perfectionistic, and they frequently come to mind on their own.

5. Examine Corresponding Beliefs:

Problem-Solving: Encourage people to investigate the underlying assumptions that underlie their habitual thinking. Examine your assumptions about acceptability, deservingness, or judgmental anxiety, for instance.

6. Practical Assessment: Analyzing the Evidence: **

Urge people to logically weigh the facts that both confirm and refute their pessimistic beliefs. Exist additional impartial viewpoints or other explanations?

7. Reducing the worst-case scenario: Examine the implications and likelihood of the feared scenario in a realistic manner to counteract catastrophic thinking. What is the worst-case scenario, and how likely is it to occur?

8. Cognitive Restructuring:

Generating Alternative Thoughts: Encourage others to come up with more realistic and well-balanced alternative ideas. Urge them to examine a more impartial and caring perspective.

9. Affirmative Statements:

Positive Affirmations: Assist people in creating affirmations that are uplifting in order to combat negative thinking. Strengths, resiliency, and good attributes should be highlighted in these affirmations.

10. Behavioral Experiments:

Assumptions for Testing: Urge people to experiment with their actions to see if their negative beliefs are true. Participating in real-world social interactions can yield tangible proof that refutes illogical views.

11. Evaluating Historical Data:

Surveying Patterns: Examine previous events to find thought and behavior patterns. Have your pessimistic beliefs always been true, or have there been times when things worked out differently?

12. Selective Social Situation Exposure:

Exposure Counseling: One useful strategy to combat negative thinking is to include exposure to social settings that cause anxiety. People can test and adjust their views in real-world situations through gradual exposure.

13. Guided Inquiry:

Socratic Questioning: Make use of Socratic questioning to assist people in investigating the rational underpinnings of their ideas. To encourage self-discovery, encourage open-ended inquiries.

14. Maintaining a Harmonious Thought Journal:

Idea: Establish a balanced thought journal in which participants note their initial negative thinking, their alternative thoughts, and their subsequent feelings. This journal helps to monitor development.

15. Review and Introspection:

Cascade of Feedback: Examine how beneficial it is to confront negative thoughts on a regular basis. Examine how your thought processes, feelings, and actions have changed. Adapt tactics in response to criticism.

Cognitive Reframing and Perspective Shifts

Cognitive reframing is the deliberate alteration of a person's perspective and interpretation of events. This strategy seeks to replace negative thought patterns with more realistic and balanced viewpoints in the context of social anxiety. This is a manual for encouraging viewpoint changes and cognitive reframing:

1. Awareness of Negative Thoughts:

Mindfulness: Develop an awareness of detrimental ideas that you may have about social circumstances. People who practice mindfulness are able to watch their thoughts without passing judgment.

2. Fight Default Negative Thoughts:

Recognition: Determine the unfavorable automatic ideas that come with social anxiety. Raise doubts about these ideas' veracity and consider other possible explanations.

3. Objective Assessment:

Reality Testing: Urge people to logically weigh the facts that both confirm and refute their pessimistic beliefs. Are these ideas supported by any actual data?

4. Desacralizing:

The Worst-Case Situation: Examine the implications and likelihood of the feared scenario in a realistic manner to counteract catastrophic thinking. What is the worst-case scenario, and how likely is it to occur?

5. Practice Gratitude:

Attention to the Positive: Include an appreciation routine to help you refocus on the good things that come from social encounters. Motivate people to recognize and value their good moments.

6. Reflection on Strengths and Accomplishments:

constructive introspection: encourage people to consider their past successes and areas of strength. This dispels self-doubt and promotes confidence.

7. Self-Talk: Positive

Affirmations: Create uplifting affirmations to offset pessimistic ideas. The emphasis of these affirmations ought to be on one's assets, fortitude, and capacity for handling difficulties.

8. Reframing Dreadful Thoughts:

A Different Viewpoint: Motivate people to reconsider negative ideas by taking into account different viewpoints. What other perspective might there be on the matter?

9. Experimental Behavior:

Assumptions for Testing: To determine whether negative beliefs are valid, do behavioral studies. Exposure to social circumstances in real life might yield tangible proof that refutes illogical assumptions.

10. Journal of Social Success:

Supportive Feedback: No matter how tiny, record your social accomplishments in a journal. Reevaluating happy memories on a regular basis aids in perception modification.

11. Comparative Evaluation:

Surveying Patterns: Examine previous social experiences to find good trends and situations when unfavorable forecasts were not realized.

12. Turn the Script:

Hypothetical Reversal: Urge others to consider the subject from an alternative viewpoint. What would people think if the roles were reversed?

13. Practice Self-Compassion: Be Kind to Yourself: Encourage self-compassion by recognizing that everyone has difficulties and makes mistakes. Be kind to yourself like you would a friend.

14. Observational Learning:

Social Learning and Role Models: Recognize and investigate others' positive social relationships. Realize that social skills are things that can be acquired and developed over time.

15. Positive Imagery:

Future Positive Visualization: Help people envision successful outcomes in social situations in the future. Encourage them to visualize themselves interacting with others with assurance.

16. Cognitive Reframing Integrated with Exposure:

Thought Restructuring during Exposure: Use cognitive reframing strategies when confronted with social settings that cause anxiety. Immediately confront negative thoughts to increase efficacy.

17. Continuous Evaluation and Modification:

Modifying Approaches: Evaluate the efficacy of cognitive reframing strategies on a regular basis. Adapt and improve tactics in response to continuous feedback and shifts in cognitive processes.

Building a Positive and Realistic Self-Image

1. Introspection and Acceptance of Oneself:

Mindfulness Exercise: Develop self-awareness by practicing mindfulness. Encourage people to notice their feelings and ideas without passing judgment in order to promote self-acceptance.

2. Automatic Thought Analysis:

Identify and Challenge Negative Self-Talk: Acknowledge the negative self-talk linked to social anxiety. Methodically refute and reinterpret these ideas to make them more reasonable and helpful.

3. Accomplishments and Strengths List:

Introspective Task: Ask people to make a list of their accomplishments and personal assets. This practice highlights abilities and creates a feeling of achievement.

4. Self-Talk and Affirmations:

Gratitude Statements: Create affirmations that emphasize your perseverance, strengths, and positive attributes. To support a positive self-image, regularly employ constructive self-talk.

5. Behavioral Experiments for Positive Validation
Validation by Actions: Test your positive views of yourself by conducting behavioral experiments. Exposure

to social settings in real life can offer proof in favor of a positive self-perception.

6. Success Visualization:

Gracious Imagery: Assist people in visualizing productive social relationships. This mental practice fosters optimistic expectations for upcoming events.

7. Equivalency Analysis:

Emphasizing Developments: Compare your present skills and accomplishments to your prior knowledge. Celebrate and acknowledge improvement and growth.

8. Positive Reinforcement and Feedback:

Support: During treatment sessions, give constructive criticism and encouragement. Acknowledge accomplishments and efforts to support a positive self-perception.

9. Social Education and Mentors:

Information Gathering: Recognize good role models in social contexts. Emphasize the fact that practice and observation can help people acquire and develop better social skills.

10. Practice Gratitude: Prioritize positivity. Include an appreciation routine to help you refocus on the good things in life. Develop an appreciation for your unique traits and fulfilling experiences.

11. Achievable Milestones:

Realistic Goal Setting: Work together to establish reasonable societal objectives. Honor little accomplishments and utilize them as stepping stones toward greater confidence.

12. Journal of Positive Self-Image:

Recording Positive Thoughts: Urge people to write in their journals about their accomplishments and positive self-perceptions. Examine and update this journal on a regular basis.

13. Narrative Rewriting:

Social Success Stories: Examine previous social interactions and present them as achievements. Highlight the good qualities and inner assets that came through in those exchanges.

14. Gratifying Social Input:

Requesting Input: Urge people to ask dependable friends or family members for their opinions. A more accurate and favorable self-image is influenced by positive feedback.

15. Perspective on Continual Self-Growth:

Accept Growth: Encourage an attitude of ongoing self-improvement. Emphasize that social skills are dynamic and that, with effort and practice, they may be developed over time.

16. Integration with Social Skills Training and Exposure: Repeated Use: During social skills training and exposure sessions, reinforce your positive self-perceptions. Applying constructive self-talk consistently improves these therapies' efficacy.

17. Continuous Evaluation and Modification:

Modifying Approaches: Review your development of a positive self-image on a regular basis. Adapt tactics in response to continuing feedback and shifts in one's own perception.

CHAPTER SIX

MINDFULNESS AND ACCEPTANCE IN SOCIAL ANXIETY

Mindfulness-Based Interventions

When it comes to treating social anxiety, mindfulness-based interventions work well because they encourage emotional control, nonjudgmental observation, and present-moment awareness. Incorporating mindfulness into therapy approaches helps improve people's capacity to control their anxiety and interact with others more skillfully. An examination of mindfulness-based therapies is provided below:

1. A Brief Overview of Mindfulness:

Basic Knowledge: Start by clearly defining mindfulness as the discipline of being totally present in the here and now without passing judgment.

2. Intentional Breathing Exercises:

Stillness: Instruct people in mindful breathing techniques to help them focus on their breathing. This technique eases anxiety and encourages relaxation.

3. Sensory Awareness:

Body Scan Meditation: Lead people in body scan meditations, guiding them to consciously look for sensations throughout their bodies. This promotes alertness and calmness.

4. Observation of Thoughts with Mindfulness:

Awareness without Judgment: Examine the discipline of objectively and impartially examining your ideas. This aids people in separating themselves from unfavorable mental habits.

5. Surrounding Methodologies:

Linkage Senses: Introduce grounding exercises that stimulate the senses and encourage present-moment awareness, including feeling the texture of an object or concentrating on background noise.

6. Love-Kindness Meditation:

Cultivating Compassion: Use loving-kindness meditation to cultivate kindness and compassion toward others and yourself, especially in social situations.

7. Emotional Acceptance:

Emotional Regulation: Help people accept and observe their feelings without passing judgment.

Controlling one's emotional reactions to social settings is made easier by mindfulness.

8. Present-Centered Exposure:

Mindful Exposure: For social anxiety, combine exposure techniques with mindfulness. Urge people to interact with others in social settings with awareness and attention to the present.

9. Mindful Self-Compassion:

Kindness Towards Oneself: Incorporate mindful self-compassion exercises to develop an understanding and compassionate mindset toward oneself, particularly during socially challenging times.

10. Real-Time Regulation:

Breath Awareness in Social Situations: Encourage people to breathe mindfully when interacting with others. This method is a useful tool for managing anxiety on the spot.

11. Consideration of Social Experiences with Mindfulness:

Awareness Following the Event: Assist people in thoughtfully considering their social experiences. Gaining an understanding of automatic ideas and emotional responses is facilitated by this introspection.

12. Mindfulness-Based Stress Reduction (MBSR):

Structured Program: Take into account implementing components of MBR to give people a thorough and organized orientation to mindfulness.

13. Present-Centered Communication:

Mindful Communication Skills: Encourage people to be totally present during conversations to highlight mindful communication. This entails paying attention and responding carefully.

14. Cognitive Restructuring Integration:

Improving Mental Adaptability: Incorporate cognitive restructuring methods with mindfulness. Because mindfulness increases cognitive flexibility, people can react to negative thoughts in a more adaptive way.

15. Considerate Goal Establishing:

Present-Centered Objectives: Assist people in establishing social goals that are present-focused and aware. This strategy promotes concentrating on the process as opposed to only the results.

16. Integrated Practice and Consistency:

Everyday Incorporation: Urge people to include mindfulness exercises in their everyday lives. Regular practice makes it easier to incorporate mindfulness into everyday life.

17. Timely Evaluation and Modification: Stitching Methodologies: Evaluate the benefits of mindfulness exercises on a regular basis. Adjust interventions according to each person's choices and changing needs.

Acceptance and Commitment Therapy (ACT)

Acceptance and Commitment Therapy (ACT) is a therapeutic strategy that helps people overcome obstacles, such as social anxiety, by combining behavioral interventions with mindfulness techniques. ACT places a strong emphasis on mindfulness, adherence to values-based behavior, and acceptance of one's thoughts and feelings. An outline of how ACT can be used to treat social anxiety is provided below:

1. Present-Moment Awareness:

Mindful Acceptance: Urge people to accept their social anxiety-related thoughts and feelings in a thoughtful, judgment-free manner. Rather than resisting these experiences, the emphasis is on recognizing and examining them.

2. Explanation of Values:

Finding the Essential Values: Assist the person in defining what really matters in their life by helping them to explore and clarify their basic principles. This procedure aids in laying the groundwork for acts that have meaning and purpose.

3. Intellectual Distortion:

Putting Your Mind at Rest: To assist people in separating themselves from upsetting ideas associated with social anxiety, teach them cognitive defusion strategies. People are able to react to these ideas more flexibly when they create distance.

4. Present-Centered Exposure:

Mindfulness-Based Exposure: Incorporate mindfulness practices into social anxiety exposure exercises. People acquire the ability to approach social circumstances with curiosity and openness, putting more emphasis on the here and now than on worries about the future.

5. Deep Action:

Ethics-Based Conduct: Assist people in committing to values-based behaviors that are consistent with their self-identified values. This entails establishing and pursuing significant and satisfying goals.

6. Emotional Regulation through Acceptance

Acceptance of Emotions: Stress the importance of embracing and allowing social anxiety-related emotions without trying to control or repress them. Emotional avoidance is lessened by this acceptance.

7. Self-Awareness as Observer:

Definition of the "Observer Self": Promote the growth of the "observer self," which calls on people to see themselves with compassion and objectivity. Self-awareness and self-compassion are fostered by this.

8. Mindful Self-Compassion Activities:

Kindness Towards Oneself: Include mindful self-compassion activities to develop a compassionate and understanding mindset toward oneself, particularly in difficult social situations.

9. Exposure Aligned with Values:

Exposure Based on Values: Create exposure exercises that are in line with the person's beliefs. This increases interest in and motivation for the exposure process.

10. Expansion and Acceptance of Inner Experience: Willingness to Experience: Encourage people to be willing to feel anxious without trying to get rid of it, as well as to increase their tolerance for discomfort. This encourages a more adaptable and open-minded approach to social circumstances.

11. Mindful Action in Social Contexts:

Present-Centered Engagement: Assist people in participating mindfully in social settings. This entails being in the moment, observing ideas objectively, and acting with intention in accordance with one's values.

12. Values-Based Objective Establishment:

Creating Intentional Objectives: Collaborate on developing goals that match the individual's values. These aspirations become driving factors for tackling social challenges.

13. Acceptance of ambiguity:

Embracing Uncertainty: Foster acceptance of ambiguity in social circumstances. This involves accepting that uncertainty is a natural element of life and does not inevitably lead to undesirable outcomes.

14. Mindfulness Practice Integration:

Whole Integration: Integrate ACT concepts with different mindfulness practices, like body scan meditations and breath awareness, to develop a comprehensive and all-encompassing approach.

15. Consistent Evaluation and Modification:

Continuous Modification: Review progress frequently and modify interventions in response to feedback and changing requirements. This guarantees that the therapy strategy stays customized to the particular experiences of the person.

Integrating Mindfulness into Cognitive Behavioral Strategies

Including mindfulness in cognitive behavioral therapy (CBT) improves the efficacy of social anxiety treatment techniques. When mindfulness exercises and cognitive behavioral therapy (CBT) are combined, a comprehensive strategy that encourages acceptance, present-moment awareness, and adaptive coping is produced. The following outlines a method for skillfully incorporating mindfulness with cognitive-behavioral techniques:

1. Methods for Mindful Grounding:

Perceptual Awareness: Practice mindful grounding at the start of sessions to improve your awareness of the present moment. To achieve a focused and serene mood, include sensory-focused techniques like body scan meditations or deep breathing.

2. Present-Centered Exposure:

Mindful Exposure and Response Prevention: Incorporate mindfulness practices into social anxiety exposure exercises. During exposures, place a strong emphasis on present-moment mindfulness to help people approach events more clearly and with less response.

3. Conscious Acceptance of Thoughts and Feelings:

Observation without Judgment: Include mindfulness in cognitive restructuring by helping people see their feelings and thoughts objectively. Place more emphasis on accepting these sensations than on quickly reorganizing your thinking.

4. Mindful Breathing during Cognitive Reorganizing:

Focused Attention: Tell people to practice mindful breathing while they are reorganizing their cognitive processes. By doing this, they are able to stay focused on the here and now and have less cognitive fusion with upsetting thoughts.

5. Aligning Goals with Values:

Values-Based Mindful Goal Setting: Incorporate mindfulness practices with goal-setting. Assist people in establishing goals that are consistent with their values and lead them to deliberately adopt behaviors that are consistent with their ideals.

6. Kindness Toward Oneself:

Mindful Self-Compassion Practices: Integrate self-compassionate techniques with cognitive-behavioral approaches. Encourage people to treat themselves with compassion and empathy when they are going through difficult times.

7. Training in Mindful Communication Skills:

Talking from the Present: Incorporate mindfulness into social skills training by stressing present-centered communication. Urge people to engage in social situations with authenticity, mindfulness, and full presence.

8. Methods of Cognitive Defusion:

Putting Your Thoughts in Perspective: Incorporate strategies for cognitive defusion into cognitive restructuring. Instruct people to observe troubling thoughts without becoming attached in order to establish a mental distance from them.

9. Conscientious Coping Plans:

In-the-Moment Coping Techniques: Create coping plans that incorporate techniques based on mindfulness. This could entail practicing grounding exercises or mindful breathing in difficult social circumstances.

10. Training for Mindful Relaxation:

Conscious Relaxation: Include mindfulness exercises in your relaxation regimen. In order to promote relaxation, teach them mindful relaxation practices that include body sensations and breath awareness.

11. Acceptance of Uncertainty in Exposure:

Embracing Uncertainty Mindfully: During exposure exercises, stress awareness is important for tolerating uncertainty. Guide individuals to be present in the moment and embrace the unpredictability inherent with social interactions.

12. Mindful Visualization for Social Success:

Positive Imagery: Integrate mindfulness into visualization exercises. Guide individuals in actively imagining good social encounters, focusing on the sensory aspects of favorable results.

13. Mindfulness in Behavioral Experiments: Present-Centered Experimentation:

Apply mindfulness during behavioral experiments. Encourage individuals to engage thoughtfully in experiments, monitoring their thoughts and feelings without judgment.

14. Mindful Review and Reflection:

Reflective Practice: Include periods of focused introspection. Encourage people to thoughtfully reflect on their experiences following exercises or exposures to help them gain self-awareness and understanding.

15. Integrating Holistic Mindfulness:

Effective Use: Make an effort to incorporate mindfulness into the therapeutic process in a seamless manner. Make sure that mindfulness exercises are integrated into cognitive-behavioral treatments rather than being used as stand-alone treatments.

CHAPTER SEVEN

MANAGING PHYSICAL SYMPTOMS OF SOCIAL ANXIETY

Relaxation Techniques and Deep Breathing

Deep breathing exercises and other relaxation methods are useful aids for social anxiety management. These techniques assist people in lowering their stress levels, controlling their bodily reactions, and developing a calmer mindset. Here's how to use deep breathing and relaxation methods with social anxiety treatment strategies:

1. Diaphragmatic Inhalation:

Targeted Breathing in the Abdomen: Instead of encouraging people to breathe shallowly from their chests, begin with diaphragmatic breathing. stress by taking calm breaths and letting them out.

2. Inhaling through the box:

Four counts Breathe in, hold, release, hold: Present box breathing as a methodical approach. Four counts are made by inhaling, holding, exhaling, and holding the breath. Relaxation and rhythmic breathing are encouraged by this technique.

3. Introduction to Progressive Muscle Relaxation (PMR): Muscle Relaxation Systematic: Include PMR by instructing people to tension and then release specific muscle groups. This technique aids in easing the general tenseness in the muscles brought on by anxiety.

4. Present-Moment Focus:

Mindful Breathing: Encourage people to concentrate on their breathing sensations, such as the sensation of air moving through their nose or the rise and fall of their chest, to incorporate mindfulness into deep breathing.

5. Directed Visualization:

Relaxation Visualization: To conjure up peaceful mental images, practice guided visualization. Help people visualize serene settings while using all of their senses to help them relax.

6. Breathing:

4-7-8 Breathe in for four, hold it for seven, and then exhale for eight: Instruct them in the 4-7-8 breathing method, which involves inhaling for four counts, holding their breath for seven, and then exhaling for eight. This exercise encourages long, relaxing exhaled breaths.

7. Body Scan Meditation:

Systematic Body Awareness: Introduce body scan meditation, which helps people to consciously release any tight spots in their bodies and mindfully scan their bodies for tension.

8. Square Breathing:

Side lengths are equal: Encourage people to breathe in, hold, release, and repeat in a square pattern for equal intervals of time. This breathing technique improves focus and relaxation.

9. Self-calming Technique:

Emphasis on Autogenic Statements: Encourage people to repeat words that connote warmth and weight in order to teach them how to relax and become peaceful.

10.Counting Breaths:

Emphasize breath counting: Include breath counting as a basic method. Teach them to count their breaths to help divert their focus from worrying thoughts.

11. Easy Body Unwinding:

Tensed and Released: Encourage people to rapidly tighten and then release different muscle groups to induce a rapid relaxation response while they are experiencing elevated anxiety.

12. A Different Method of Nostril Breathing:

Managing Breath: Encourage people to breathe through one nostril, exhale through the other, and vice versa by introducing them to alternate nostril breathing. This exercise encourages calmness and equilibrium.

13. Belly Breathing with Visualization:

Using imagery to unwind: Combine belly breathing with visualization. Give them instructions to visualize breathing in peace and out of tension, synchronizing the breath with the visualization.

14. Awareness of Breath in Social Circumstances:

Breathing During Exposure Consciously: Stress how important it is to breathe mindfully in social situations. Tell them to pay attention to their breath in order to remain grounded and in the moment.

15. Daily Routine and Integration:

Include in Your Everyday Routine: Promote the consistent application of relaxation techniques as a daily habit, rather than reserving them for times when anxiety is at its highest. Practice on a regular basis improves effectiveness.

Cognitive-Behavioral Interventions for Physical Symptoms

Treatments for social anxiety symptoms that are successful in treating physical symptoms include cognitive-behavioral therapy (CBT). Through addressing the mind-body connection, these techniques seek to reduce the physical symptoms associated with anxiety. This is a manual on CBT techniques designed especially for the physical symptoms of social anxiety:

1. Mind-Body Connection Education:

Recognizing Physical Reactions: Start by teaching people about the relationship that exists between ideas, feelings, and bodily experiences. Assist them in realizing the bodily responses that anxiety elicits.

2.Restructuring the Mind to Avoid Catastrophic Thoughts:

Dispelling Dreadful Thoughts: Determine and confront debilitating ideas associated with somatic manifestations. Encourage people to recast distorted perceptions of their bodies into more realistic ones.

3. Body Scan Based on Mindfulness:

Knowledge of Physical Sensations: Incorporate a body scan practice with mindfulness. Encourage people to scan their bodies thoughtfully, focusing on the feelings they experience without passing judgment, in order to promote acceptance and awareness.

4. Introduction to Tangible Senses: Exposure to symptoms Gradually: Create exposure activities that are tailored to address bodily complaints. People can become accustomed to and endure body reactions by being gradually exposed to situations that cause them to experience them.

5. Behavioral Tests Using Sensations of the Body:

Examining Worried Forecasts: Conduct behavioral tests to evaluate nervous assumptions about physical symptoms. Urge them to participate fully in the circumstances so they can see the real effects on their bodies.

6. Grounding Methodologies:

Strategies with a Sensory Focus: In order to divert focus from bodily discomfort, teach grounding skills. These could be sensation textures, concentrating on the breath, or moving in a rhythmic manner to help people stay in the present.

7. Biofeedback Instructions:

Keeping an eye on and controlling physiological responses: Describe the use of biofeedback as a method for monitoring and controlling physiological reactions. People who receive this instruction are able to consciously regulate some body functions.

8. Attaining Physical Comfort with Positive Visualization:

Using imagery to unwind: Help people visualize situations in which their bodily problems are minimal by encouraging them to use positive imagery. This can assist in forming an association in the mind between particular situations and decreasing discomfort levels.

9. Physical Sensations That Decatastrophize:

Thoughts on Testing Reality: Motivate people to de-stigmatize bodily experiences by evaluating the possibility and ramifications of their imagined scenarios with objectivity. Assist them in gaining a more grounded viewpoint.

**10. Physical Relaxation Through Mindful Breathing:
Methods of Conscious Breathing:** Instruct students in mindful breathing as a calming method. Give them instructions on how to combat physiological arousal by concentrating on taking deliberate, slow breaths.

11. Training in Social Skills with an Emphasis on Relaxation:

Bringing Relaxation and Skill Development Together: Combine relaxing techniques with social skills training. Assist people in practicing social skills and using ways to manage physical discomfort at the same time.

12. Gradual Exposure to Triggers:

Systematic Desensitization to Physical Triggers: Employ a methodical desensitization process by introducing people to circumstances or stimuli linked to bodily symptoms one at a time. This methodical technique helps to lessen anxiety reactions.

**13. Contemplation Logs for Tangible Symptoms:
Monitoring and Prompting Thoughts:** Use thought records to track and confront thoughts related to physical problems. Guide folks to explore evidence supporting and refuting their fearful feelings.

14. Acceptance and Mindful Coping Plans: Embracing Physical Reactions: Encourage acceptance of bodily reactions by assisting people in creating thoughtful coping mechanisms. Urge them to approach circumstances with an acceptance of their bodies and their sensations.

15. Ongoing Evaluation and Modification:

Changing Techniques: Evaluate the success of interventions on a regular basis and modify them in response to feedback and modifications in the person's experience. Make sure that tactics continue to be adapted to their changing requirements.

Medication and its Role in Social Anxiety Treatment

For patients with social anxiety disorder (SAD), medication can play a significant role in the treatment regimen, particularly when paired with psychotherapy techniques. Note that when symptoms severely interfere with day-to-day functioning, or in cases of moderate to severe social anxiety, medication is usually taken into consideration. Below is a detailed summary of how medicine is used to treat social anxiety:

1. First-Line Medications:

Selective Serotonin Reuptake Inhibitors (SSRIs): For treating social anxiety, SSRIs, including paroxetine, sertraline, and fluoxetine, are frequently recommended as first-line treatments. They function by raising serotonin levels in the brain, which aid with mood and anxiety regulation.

2. An Alternative to Serotonin-Norepinephrine Reuptake Inhibitors (SNRIs): In cases where SSRIs are not completely successful, SNRIs like venlafaxine may be administered. They also raise serotonin levels and affect norepinephrine, which helps stabilize mood.

3. Benzodiazepines:

Temporary Relief: Clonazepam and lorazepam are two examples of benzodiazepines that can be used to temporarily relieve acute anxiety symptoms. But because of the possibility of dependence, they are usually not used over an extended period of time.

4. Alpha-Blockers:

Handling Physiologic Indications: Propranolol is one of the beta-blockers used to treat the physiological signs of anxiety, like tremors and an accelerated heartbeat.

They are frequently used for situational anxiety on an as-needed basis.

5. Inhibitors of Monoamine Oxidase (MAOIs): Not as Frequently Ascribed: Due to dietary limitations and possible drug interactions, MAOIs like phenelzine are used less frequently. If alternative therapies don't work, they might be taken into consideration.

6. Combinations of Antidepressants:

Combined Methods: Sometimes a combination of drugs is recommended, including an augmentation with a low-dose atypical antipsychotic or an SSRI plus benzodiazepine for momentary symptom alleviation.

7. Personalized Treatment Plans:

Customized Methods: Individualized medicine decisions are made in response to various circumstances, including the degree of symptoms, the existence of co-occurring diseases, and the patient's reaction to particular drugs.

8. Upkeep and Extended Usage:

Extended-Term Aspects: Even though SSRIs and SNRIs are frequently used over an extended period of time, the patient and their healthcare provider should work together to determine how long to take a medicine.

9. Tolerability and Side Effects:

Observation and Modifications: Healthcare professionals regularly check for adverse effects and modify prescription schedules as necessary. It's critical that people voice any worries or negative reactions right away.

10. Gradual Action Onset:

Treatment with Patience: A number of social anxiety drugs take several weeks to fully manifest their therapeutic benefits. It is important to exercise patience in the early stages of treatment.

11. Withdrawal and Discontinuation:

Progressive Tapering: In order to reduce withdrawal symptoms, stopping medication should be done under the supervision of a healthcare provider. This is frequently accomplished through a progressive tapering approach.

12. Therapeutic Partnership:

Cooperation with Counselor: Choosing to take medicine is frequently decided in consultation with a psychiatrist or therapist. Ensuring complete and thorough care is contingent upon the presence of a therapeutic partnership.

13. In conjunction with psychotherapy:

Increased Efficiency: Psychotherapy, particularly cognitive-behavioral therapy (CBT), which tackles the cognitive distortions and behavioral patterns linked to social anxiety, is frequently more beneficial when paired with medication.

14. Ongoing Follow-Up Meetings:

Continuous Observation: It is imperative to schedule routine follow-up consultations with healthcare specialists in order to track advancement, evaluate side effects, and modify the treatment plan as needed.

15. Education and Empowerment of Patients: Making Informed Decisions: Giving patients comprehensive information about the drug, its possible advantages, and its drawbacks gives them the power to decide on their own course of treatment.

CHAPTER EIGHT

RELAPSE PREVENTION AND MAINTENANCE STRATEGIES

Identifying Triggers for Social Anxiety Relapse

Maintaining improvement and avoiding setbacks require an understanding of the triggers that lead to social anxiety recurrence. By recognizing these triggers, people can create preventative plans and coping techniques. The following list of frequent triggers for relapses in social anxiety can be used as a guide:

1. Big Life Shifts:

Adjustments and Transitions: Due to the stress and adjustment needed, big life changes like starting a new career, relocating to a new location, or drastically changing one's lifestyle can cause social anxiety recurrence.

2. Comparative Social Analysis:

Negative Self-Relatedness: Excessive social comparison, particularly on social media, can exacerbate feelings of inadequacy and lead to a relapse in social anxiety. Unrealistic standards are typically the result of unhealthy comparisons.

3. Achievement Standards:

Elevated Anticipations and Assessor Fear: Rekindling social anxiety can be caused by having unreasonably high expectations for oneself or by worrying about receiving a poor rating when performing. Anxiety is exacerbated by the need to live up to perceived norms.

4. Denial or Disapproval:

Fear of Being Turned Down: Even mild rejection or criticism can set off a relapse in social anxiety. The dread of being disapproved of or judged by others may be heightened by unpleasant past experiences.

5. Isolation from Society:

Removal from Social Networks: Long-term social disengagement or retreat from social activities can exacerbate anxiety about re-entering the social world and lead to the decline of social skills.

6. Informal Social Circumstances:

Inconsistency: Social anxiety can be triggered by unstructured social encounters when the outcome is uncertain. An atmosphere of uncertainty and unease can be exacerbated by unclear expectations.

7. A Negative Dialogue with Yourself: Internal Recommendations: Negative self-talk and self-critical thinking can damage one's sense of self and cause a relapse in social anxiety. It's important to recognize these ideas and challenge them.

8. Sensory Evaluation:

Awaiting the verdict: A major cause of social anxiety relapse is the fear of being poorly evaluated by others. This can appear in both official and casual social contexts.

9. Experiences with Social Rejection:

Previous Adverse Events: Triggers may reappear in the form of past trauma or social rejection experiences. These recollections could make you more anxious in similar circumstances.

10. Coercion to Adhere:

Apprehension of Deviation: Anxiety can be sparked by pressure to live up to social norms or expectations, particularly if there seems to be a disconnect between one's own values and those of society.

11. Impractical Social Expectations:

Aiming for Excellence: In particular, when faced with obstacles or making mistakes, setting unattainable expectations for social interactions and expecting perfect performance might pave the way for a relapse in social anxiety.

12. Unfavorable Comments:

Fear of Adverse Reactions: Increased social anxiety can be caused in part by the fear of hearing unfavorable comments or criticism from others, whether those comments are imagined or genuine.

13. Insufficient Social Support:

Solitary and Unsupported: Relapses in social anxiety may be more likely to occur in situations where one feels alone or without a support system. A heightened anxiety about social interactions can result from a lack of social relationships.

14. Intense Performance Requirement:

Excessive Focus on Results: Overemphasizing the results of social interactions over the process itself can lead to a relapse in social anxiety and increase performance pressure.

15. Impaired Social Encounters:

Current Unfavorable Exchanges: One's perspective on social encounters can be affected by recent unfavorable social experiences, whether they occurred offline or online, and this can exacerbate anticipatory anxiety.

Avoidance-Based Coping Techniques:

- **Mindfulness and Self-Compassion:** Learn self-compassion and mindfulness exercises to help you deal with difficult feelings and thoughts.
- **Gradual Exposure:** To develop resilience and gradually desensitize triggers, gradually expose yourself to social situations that you find frightening.
- **Social Skills Training:** To increase confidence in a variety of social situations, regularly practice and improve social skills.
- **Cognitive Restructuring:** Recognize and confront skewed ideas associated with triggers, encouraging more pragmatic and optimistic thinking.
- **Seeking Support:** Create a network of support and be honest about difficulties with family, friends, or a mental health professional.

Developing a Relapse Prevention Plan

One of the most important tools for people managing social anxiety is a relapse prevention plan. It facilitates the identification of possible triggers, the development of coping mechanisms, and the creation of a maintenance plan. This is a thorough how-to guide for creating a plan to avoid relapse:

1. Introspection:

Determine Your Own Triggers: Think back on previous encounters and pinpoint certain circumstances or incidents that have caused social anxiety. This could include situations in social settings, ideas, or actions that exacerbate anxiety.

2. Warning Indications:

Acknowledge Early Signs: Identify the early warning indicators of a possible relapse. These symptoms could be behavioral, emotional, or bodily clues to elevated anxiety.

3. Vulnerabilities and Triggers:

Enumerate possible triggers: Make a note of the situations, ideas, or actions that might lead to elevated anxiety levels as probable social anxiety triggers.

4. Strategies for Coping:

Determine workable coping mechanisms: Enumerate coping mechanisms that have been successful in reducing social anxiety. These could be mindfulness exercises, cognitive restructuring, relaxation techniques, or asking for help from others.

5. Network of Social Support:

Create support systems: Find people in your social support network who are able to provide comprehension, inspiration, and support when things get tough. Convey your requirements and assemble a solid support network.

6. Expert Assistance:

Keep in Touch with Your Therapist: If you are receiving therapy, talk to your therapist about creating a strategy to prevent relapses. Continue holding regular meetings to discuss issues and make necessary strategy adjustments.

7. Aim Establishment:

Establish attainable and realistic goals: Set both short- and long-term objectives for your social relationships. These objectives ought to be reasonable, well-defined, and consistent with the person's values.

8. Monitoring Progress:

Regularly Assess Progress: Put in place a mechanism for routinely evaluating how well goals are being met and identifying any areas that could need more work or modification.

9. Well-Being Lifestyle Practices:

Make self-care a priority: Stress the value of leading a healthy lifestyle that includes getting enough sleep, working out frequently, and eating a balanced diet. Emotional resilience is influenced by physical well-being.

10. Meditation Techniques:

Include mindfulness practices: Include mindfulness exercises in your everyday routine. Practicing mindfulness fosters a nonjudgmental acceptance of thoughts and feelings as well as a greater sense of self-awareness.

11. Activation of Behavior:

Take part in intentional activities: Activate your behavior by doing things that make you happy and give you a sense of success. This mitigates the tendency toward withdrawal and isolation.

12. Coping Strategy for Emergencies:

Create contingency plans: Make a detailed plan for handling sudden, severe anxiety attacks. A list of emergency coping mechanisms or contact details for prompt assistance may be included.

13. Conventional Check-Ins: Plan Frequent Self-Check-Ins:

Make time on a regular basis to evaluate your emotional health and social anxiety level. Based on these self-check-ins, modify your plan as necessary.

14. Methods of Relaxation:

Include Calming Activities: Include methods of relaxation in your practice, such as progressive muscle relaxation or deep breathing. Frequent practice can help reduce anxiety in general.

15. Solicited Assistance:

Honor accomplishments: No matter how tiny, acknowledge and celebrate your accomplishments. Good behaviors are reinforced, and a sense of success is fostered by positive reinforcement.

16. Accessibility and Documentation:

Make a plan in writing. Write out the relapse prevention strategy. For further responsibility, make it easily accessible and distribute it to reliable people in your support system.

17. Contacts for Emergencies:

Gather emergency phone numbers: Have a list of emergency contacts on hand that includes friends, family, and mental health providers. This guarantees prompt access to assistance in times of need.

18. Monthly Plan Evaluation:

Review of the Scheduled Plan: Plan on reviewing the relapse prevention strategy on a frequent basis and making necessary adjustments based on new needs, experiences, and input from support systems.

Modification Techniques:

Adaptability and Flexibility: Stress the value of adaptability when making strategy adjustments. Since social anxiety is a dynamic condition, the efficacy of the plan is increased when coping mechanisms are flexible.

Long-Term Strategies for Maintaining Progress

Adopting long-term tactics that promote ongoing growth and resilience is necessary to maintain progress in the management of social anxiety. These tactics seek to bring about long-lasting, constructive transformation rather than just temporary coping methods. This is a thorough guide to long-term tactics for sustaining advancement.

1. Ongoing Therapeutic Interaction:

Frequent Therapy Sessions: Continue to see a mental health professional on a frequent basis, such as a counselor or therapist. Regular therapy tackles new issues, offers continuing support, and strengthens the coping mechanisms that have been taught.

2. Introspection and Self-Monitoring:

Continuous Self-Examination: Encourage the practice of introspection and self-reflection. Assess social anxiety-related thoughts, feelings, and behaviors on a regular basis. Determine trends, achievements, and opportunities for development.

3. Improving Social Skills:

Ongoing Skills Improvement: Maintain your progress in developing social skills by practicing regularly. Take part in activities that facilitate constructive social interactions, as they can lead to a rise in self-assurance and skill.

4. Gradual Challenges and Exposure: Gradually expose yourself to social circumstances that test your anxiety tolerance. To reduce anxiety and increase tolerance, do exposure exercises on a regular basis.

5. Meditation and Mindfulness:

Integrated Techniques for Mindfulness: Include meditation and mindfulness exercises in your everyday routine. Develop an awareness of the current moment to reduce stress, improve emotional control, and improve general wellbeing.

6. Daily Schedule for Physical Activity:

Frequent Exercise: Keep up a regular exercise schedule. Exercise has been shown to improve mental health by lowering anxiety and enhancing wellbeing.

7. Healthy Living Options

Healthy Eating and Sleep: Give adequate sleep and a well-balanced diet first priority. Maintaining a healthy lifestyle has a positive impact on mood and cognitive performance, as well as resilience overall.

8. Affirmations of Positivity:

Everyday Declarations: Make using positive affirmations a part of your everyday routine. Positive self-beliefs can be strengthened by affirmations, which also serve to offset negative self-talk linked to social anxiety.

9. Ongoing Instruction:

Remain Up to Date: Learn about cognitive-behavioral techniques, mental wellness, and social anxiety. Being knowledgeable gives you the ability to make wise decisions regarding your health.

10. Maintenance of Social Support:

Nurture Relationships: Sustain and cultivate a positive rapport. Maintain regular contact with loved ones and speak candidly about your experiences. Having a solid support network is essential.

11. Adaptability and Flexibility:

Adapt to Change: Accept adaptability and flexibility in your social anxiety management strategy. When conditions change, strategies that worked well in the past might need to be adjusted.

12. Goal Setting and Achievement:

Continuous Goal Setting: Set new goals connected with personal beliefs. Regularly achieve and celebrate these goals, fostering a sense of accomplishment and motivating further progress.

13. Volunteering and Community Engagement:

Community Contribution: Take part in volunteer work or other community-related activities. Adding to a greater good can strengthen social ties and give one a sense of purpose.

14. Reflection and Journaling:

Thought Diary: Keep a mental notebook to record encounters, difficulties, and achievements. Learning and self-awareness are reinforced as you reflect on your journey.

15. Practices of Self-Compassion:

Develop self-compassion: Make self-compassion a regular practice. During difficult times, be gentle and understanding with yourself. Resilience and a positive self-image are fostered by self-compassion.

16. Applying Acquired Skills:

Utilize Acquired Skills: Integrate the cognitive-behavioral abilities gained into everyday life. Regularly apply tactics such as cognitive restructuring and behavioral exposure to real-world circumstances.

17. Consistent Progress Review:

Regular Review of Progress: Plan regular evaluations of your development. Honor successes, recognize development, and point out areas that still need work. Self-awareness is improved when progress reviews are conducted proactively.

18. Long-Term Integration of Lifestyle:

Adapt Strategies to Your Lifestyle: Make sure your daily routine incorporates techniques for handling social anxiety. In order to achieve sustainable improvement, coping strategies and constructive behaviors must become second nature.

CHAPTER NINE

CASE STUDIES AND PRACTICAL APPLICATIONS

Application of CBT Techniques in Real-Life Scenarios

Techniques from cognitive-behavioral therapy (CBT) are useful and efficient instruments for handling a range of difficulties in everyday situations. Here are some scenarios in which you can use important CBT techniques:

1. Context: Anxiety About Public Speaking

CBT Method: Cognitive Restructuring

Utilization: Recognize and address any unfavorable ideas you may have about public speaking. Think more realistic and balanced thoughts instead of self-defeating ones. Rather than thinking, "I'll embarrass myself," try framing it as, "I can handle this, and everyone makes mistakes."

2. Context: Social Event

CBT Method: Behavioral Exposure Anxiety

Utilization: Introduction to social situations gradually. Attend smaller events initially, then work your way up to larger ones. Over time, this helps to desensitize anxiety and boost self-assurance.

3. Context: Avoidance and Procrastination

CBT Method: Behavioral Activation

Utilization: Divide up the work into smaller, more doable steps. Make a timetable with daily objectives in mind. You can resist the strong temptation to put things off by concentrating on one task at a time.

4. Context: Adverse Self-Talk at Work

CBT Method: Thought Logs

Utilization: To monitor your negative thoughts at work, keep a thought journal. Recognize trends and confront erroneous assumptions. Take "I'll never succeed" as an example; instead, say, "I may face challenges, but I have the skills to overcome them."

5. Context: Anxiety-Related Sleep Disturbance

CBT Method: Relaxation Techniques

Utilization: Before going to bed, engage in deep breathing or progressive muscle relaxation. Establish a relaxing bedtime routine to let your body know when it's time to relax, which will lower anxiety and enhance the quality of your sleep.

6. Context: Relationship Conflict:

CBT Method: Communication Skills

Utilization: Express your emotions using "I" phrases to avoid placing blame. Instead of emphasizing violence, concentrate on assertiveness and active listening. Say "I feel upset when..." rather than "You always..." as an example.

7. Context: Excessive Generalization Following an Error

CBT Method: Cognitive Restructuring

Utilization: Examine the evidence to refute overly generalized statements. A mistake at work should not lead you to think, "I always mess up." Rather, accept the particular incident and seek out proof of your proficiency in other domains.

8. Context: Dating Rejection Fear

CBT Method: Behavioral Experiments

Utilization: Gradually boost the number of social interactions to test the fear of rejection. Begin with casual talks before moving on to more intimate ones. This aids in refuting and challenging illogical views.

9. Context: Sports Performance Anxiety:

CBT Method: Visualization

Utilization: Successful performances can be mentally practiced by using visualization techniques. Visualize yourself winning, concentrating on the good things in your sport. This lessens worry and boosts confidence.

10. Context: Widespread Fear of the Future

CBT Method: Mindfulness Meditation

Utilization: Remain conscious to avoid worrying about the future and to be in the moment. Pay attention to your breathing and observe your thoughts objectively. This method aids in bringing you back to the present.

11. Context: Flying Fear

CBT Method: Systematic Desensitization

Utilization: exposure to the aspects of flying gradually; begin with viewing images, move on to going to an airport, and finally take short flights. This methodical process aids in desensitizing the phobia.

12. Context: Workplace Imposter Syndrome

CBT Method: Cognitive Restructuring

Utilization: By enumerating your successes, you can dispel doubts about your expertise. Realize that you're not the only one who feels like an impostor; others can also be struggling with self-doubt.

13. Context: Panic Attack in Communal Areas

CBT Method: Grounding Methods

Utilization: During a panic episode, ground yourself by paying attention to your senses. List the following: five objects you can see, four tactile items, three auditory items, two olfactory items, and one gustatory item.

14. Context: Examination

CBT Method: Cognitive Restructuring Anxiety

Utilization: Dispel pessimistic exam-related ideas. Feelings like "I'll fail" should be replaced with more grounded ideas like "I've prepared well, and I'll do my best." To reduce anxiety, divide up your work into smaller study periods.

15. Context: Low Mood and Low Motivation

CBT Method: Behavioral Activation

Utilization: Plan enjoyable activities, even if you're not feeling very motivated. Take part in things that make you happy or give you a sense of success. Increasing activity levels gradually aids in the fight against depression symptoms.

Case Studies Illustrating Successful Social Anxiety Treatment

Case Study 1: Overcoming Social Anxiety Through CBT

Patient Profile:

Name: Sarah

Age: 28

Occupation: Marketing Professional

Main Concern: Severe social anxiety affecting work and personal life

Assessment:

Sarah presented with significant social anxiety, impacting her ability to communicate in professional settings and maintain personal relationships. She reported avoiding social events, experiencing panic attacks, and having negative self-perceptions.

CBT Intervention:

1. Cognitive Restructuring:

- Identified and challenged distorted thoughts, such as "Everyone is judging me" and "I must be perfect."

- Replace negative thoughts with more balanced and realistic ones, fostering self-compassion.

2. Exposure Therapy:

- Developed a hierarchy of social situations, starting with low-anxiety exposures (e.g., making eye contact) and progressing to higher-anxiety exposures (e.g., speaking in meetings).
- Engaged in graduated exposure exercises both in sessions and as homework assignments.

3. Social Skills Training:

- Practiced assertiveness and effective communication skills to improve interpersonal interactions.
- Received feedback and guidance on non-verbal cues and body language.

4. Mindfulness Techniques:

- Introduced mindfulness meditation to manage anxiety in the present moment.
- used mindfulness to challenge automatic negative thoughts and increase self-awareness.

Progress:

- Sarah demonstrated significant improvement in social interactions.

- Successfully participated in work meetings and networking events without overwhelming anxiety.

- Developed a support network and reported more satisfying personal relationships.

Follow-Up:

Sarah continued practicing CBT techniques independently, reinforcing her learned skills. She attended occasional booster sessions to address new challenges and refine strategies. She successfully maintained progress and reported a positive shift in her overall well-being.

Case Study 2: Navigating Social Anxiety in College

Student Profile:

Name: Alex

Age: 21

Academic Status: College Student

Main Concern: Social anxiety impacts academic performance and extracurricular engagement.

Assessment:

Alex struggled with fear of judgment from peers, avoiding class participation and social events. Academic performance suffered, and feelings of isolation intensified.

CBT Intervention:

1. Behavioral Experiments:

- Engaged in behavioral experiments to test feared outcomes, such as expressing opinions in class.
- Gradually increased participation, challenging the belief that others were negatively evaluating him.

2.Cognitive Restructuring:

- Identified and challenged cognitive distortions related to social interactions.
- Encouraged positive self-talk and reframed catastrophic thoughts about social situations.

3. Exposure Therapy:

- Developed a hierarchy of exposure tasks related to academic and social settings.
- Implemented systematic desensitization to gradually confront and overcome fears.

4. Group Therapy:

- Participated in group therapy to practice social skills in a supportive environment.
- Shared experiences with peers facing similar challenges, reducing feelings of isolation.

Progress:

- Alex experienced a notable increase in class participation and engagement in social activities.
- Improved academic performance due to increased attendance and active participation.
- Developed a sense of belonging within the college community.

Follow-Up:

Alex continued with maintenance sessions to address new stressors and refine coping strategies. He became a peer mentor for others facing social anxiety, demonstrating sustained progress and a positive impact on the college community.

Practical Tips for Individuals and Therapists Working with Social Anxiety

1.   **Self-Compassion:** Show yourself love and understanding, especially while facing difficult social circumstances, to cultivate self-compassion.

2. **Gradual Exposure:** As your confidence grows, progressively expose yourself to social circumstances that make you uncomfortable, starting with ones that cause you less anxiety.

3. **Positive Affirmations:** Use affirmations to uplift your mood and combat negative self-talk by incorporating them into your everyday routine.

4. **Mindfulness Practices**: To be present and control worry in the here and now, practice mindfulness exercises like deep breathing or mindfulness meditation.

5. **Social Skills Practice:** To increase confidence and enhance interpersonal relationships, regularly practice social skills in relaxed settings.

6.   **Aim Establishing**: Establish attainable and reasonable objectives for your social interactions. Appreciate little accomplishments and use them as inspiration to take on more difficult tasks.

7. **Healthy Lifestyle:** Make maintaining a healthy lifestyle a priority. This includes getting enough sleep, eating a

balanced diet, and exercising on a regular basis. These elements all improve general well-being.

8. Seek Support: Form a network of friends, family, or support groups so that you can talk honestly about your struggles and get help when you need it.

9. Cogitation Logs: To monitor and combat unfavorable thoughts related to social anxiety, keep a thought journal. This aids in pattern recognition and the correction of cognitive errors.

10. Expert Assistance: To obtain focused interventions and support, think about obtaining expert assistance from a therapist educated in cognitive-behavioral therapy (CBT).

Advantageous Advice for Therapists Treating Patients with Social Anxiety:

1. Personalized Treatment Plans: Given the distinctive nature of each person's experience with social anxiety, customize treatment plans to meet their particular requirements and objectives.

2. Cooperative Goal Establishment: Work together with clients to establish reasonable and doable goals for the treatment of social anxiety. Include them in the process of creating goals in order to increase engagement and motivation.

3. Psychoeducation: Clearly and thoroughly explain social anxiety, its symptoms, cognitive-behavioral components, and research-proven treatment options.

4. Exposure tactics: Adjust exposure tactics to the patient's hierarchy of social situations that they find frightening by introducing them gradually into therapy sessions.

5. Cognitive Restructuring: Lead clients through exercises related to cognitive restructuring to recognize and confront harmful thought patterns linked to social anxiety.

6. Mindfulness Integration: Include mindfulness practices in therapy to help patients become more self-aware and learn how to deal with anxiety in the here and now.

7. Behavioral Experiments: Provide clients with chances to evaluate and adjust maladaptive ideas by encouraging them to participate in behavioral experiments outside of therapy sessions.

8. Cooperative Counseling: Think of group therapy as a supplement to individual therapy, offering a peer-supported setting for social skills development.

9. Periodical Progress Assessment: Arrange for periodical evaluations to monitor development, pinpoint areas for enhancement, and tackle new issues in the treatment of social anxiety.

10. Homework Assignments: Provide clients with hands-on homework assignments that let them use newly acquired skills in authentic settings, encouraging mastery and generalization.

11. Adaptability and Flexibility: Adjust therapy strategies in accordance with the client's development, preferences, and changing requirements for social anxiety management.

12. Positive praise: To increase motivation and confidence during the therapy process, give positive praise for all accomplishments, no matter how minor.

13. Autonomy and Empowerment: Give your customers the tools they need to take charge of their own social anxiety management. Motivate them to assume responsibility for their advancement.

14. Sensitivity to Culture: Recognize the influence of cultural influences on social anxiety and exercise cultural sensitivity. Take into account cultural quirks when creating and putting treatment plans into action.

15. Ongoing Professional Growth: Keep up-to-date on the most recent findings in social anxiety research and treatment methods. Take part in ongoing professional development to improve the efficacy of therapy.

CONCLUSION

In conclusion, when it comes to treating social anxiety, cognitive-behavioral therapy, or CBT, is a ray of hope and effectiveness. By utilizing a sophisticated combination of cognitive restructuring, exposure treatment, and mindfulness practices, cognitive behavioral therapy (CBT) provides people with the means to actively transform their ideas and behaviors, in addition to helping them comprehend the complexities of their social anxiety. This therapy method is not just an intervention; rather, it is a cooperative process that enables people to face, question, and eventually transcend the limitations that social anxiety places on their lives.

CBT-illuminated success stories abound in tales of self-discovery, resilience, and confidence restored. Through exploring the underlying cognitive errors that cause social anxiety and methodically exposing people to circumstances they are afraid of, cognitive behavioral therapy (CBT) facilitates significant change. Beyond the therapeutic setting, the acquisition of new skills to navigate social landscapes has a positive impact on an individual's general well-being and interpersonal connections.

Adopting the tenets of CBT sets people and therapists on a dynamic journey characterized by empathy, introspection, and a steadfast faith in the possibility of change. The story of success over social anxiety develops together with the therapeutic relationship, showing how people may change the course of their social interactions and pave the way for a life that is more self-assured and satisfying with the correct support and techniques.